The Story of a Special Day
Volume 352

December
17

The 351st day of the year (352nd in leap years). There are 14 days remaining until the end of the year.

by Michael Dobson

Timespinner
Press

This book is also available in e-book form for Kindle, e-pub devices, and other formats from your favorite online booksellers.

For more information about the series, about us, or about your special day, please email us at editor@timespinnerpress.com.

Look for other volumes in *The Story of a Special Day,* coming often. See www.timespinnerpress.com for details and for the most recent information.

Table of Contents

For the definition of "O.S.," "N.S.," "CE," and "BCE" used with some dates , see the section "On Names and Dates."

Cover: The Wright brothers make their first flight, December 17, 1903 — the **Cover Story and Event of the Day**. (Photo: John T. Daniels)

Quote of the Day

"When once you have tasted flight, you will forever walk the earth with your eyes turned skyward, for there you have been, and there you will always long to return."

Leonardo da Vinci

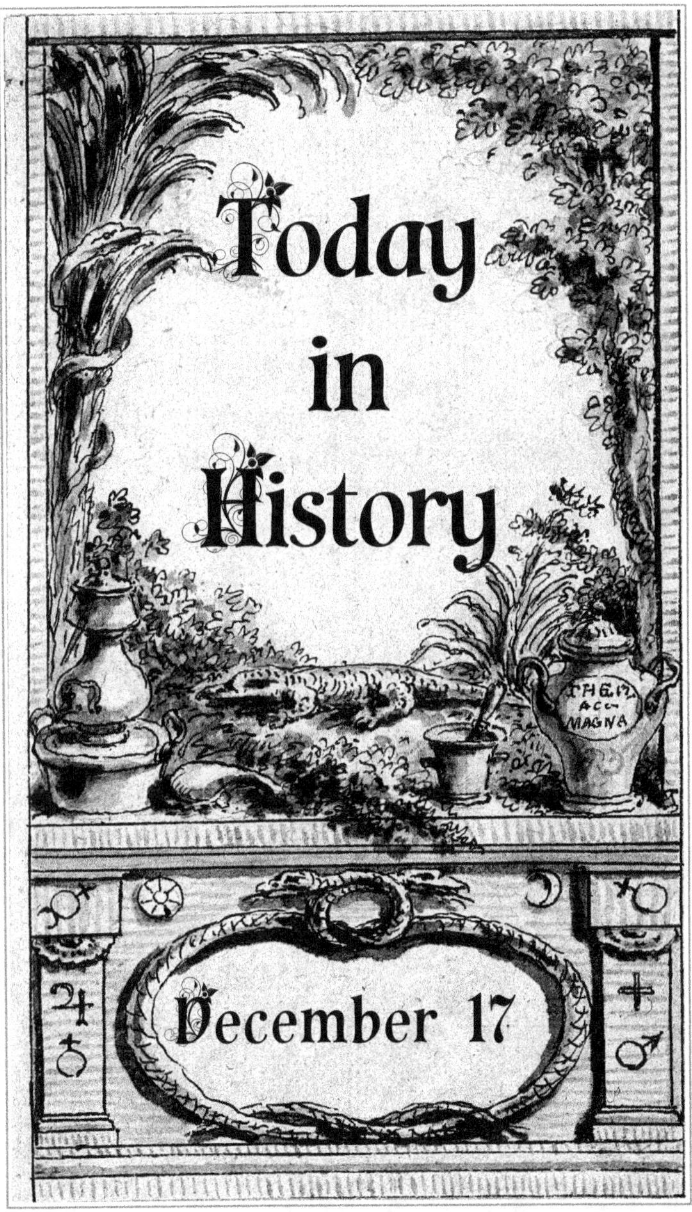
Today
in
History
December 17

December, Simon Bening (c. 1510)

What Happened on December 17?

While some days of the year are more famous than others, every day of the year is filled with important, exciting, and unusual events, from religious awakenings to natural disasters, from wars to breakthroughs in technology, and from tragedy to triumph.

In this section, you'll learn about all the events that make December 17 important, including the special event that makes up our cover story or event of the day. Some events you may already know about, others may be new to you, but all of them are important parts of the history of the work.

Let's explore some of the reasons why December 17 is a very special day!

An autographed postcard of the Wright brothers in 1908. Orville Wright is on the left, and Wilbur Wright on the right.

Event of the Day/Cover Story
1903 — The Wright Brothers Fly

On December 17, 1903, a few miles south of the town of Kitty Hawk, North Carolina, the Wright brothers made the first successful heavier-than-air flight.

Pilot Orville Wright took off in the Wright Flyer at 10:35 am, into a headwind with gusts up to 27 mph, and flew 120 feet in twelve seconds, reaching an altitude of 10 feet and achieving a ground speed of a little less than 7 miles per hour.

The Wrights flew three more times that day. The last flight covered a bit more than 850 feet, but the airplane began to pitch and crashed. Wilbur Wright, the pilot, was not injured. From these humble beginnings the age of powered flight began.

The Wright brothers grew up in Indiana and moved to Dayton, Ohio. The move interrupted their education, and neither brother finished high school. They founded a bicycle repair shop, and eventually launched their own brand. Both had become interested in flight, and used their bicycle business to support their aviation experiments.

The Wright brothers focused on the problems involved in controlling an aircraft, using birds as inspiration. They built a series of gliders, testing them at Kitty Hawk, and pioneered the use of wind tunnels for aviation research.

After the success of their glider flights in 1902, they began working on a powered version, using a lightweight engine built by their shop mechanic, Charlie Taylor. The whole plane cost less than $1,000.

Initially, newspapers ignored the press releases the Wrights sent out, but other aviation experts took notice. It was not until 1908 that the brothers began making public flights, including the first hour-long flight.

The Wrights became involved in a series of lawsuits about their patent for an airplane, as well as a feud with the Smithsonian Institution, who gave the honor of the first "capable of heavier-than-air" aircraft to Samuel Langley, who happened to be Secretary of the Smithsonian.

The Wright brothers testing a glider at Kitty Hawk, October 10, 1902

As a result, the Wrights donated the repaired 1903 plane to the London Science Museum, refusing to let it return to the US unless the Smithsonian gave the Wrights appropriate credit. It returned to the US and went on public display on December 17, 1948.

While the Wrights are generally acknowledged as the first to achieve controlled manned heavier-than-air flight, the claim remains somewhat controversial. Brazil claims its own Alberto Santos-Dumont as the first succesful aviator (he first flew in 1906), and some champion Gustave Whitehead.

Wilbur Wright died on May 30, 1912, at the age of 45. Orville lived another 35 years, and died January 30, 1948. He made his last airplane flight in 1944, aboard a Lockheed Constellation, where he observed that the wingspan of that airplane was longer than the distance of his first flight. Both brothers are buried in Dayton, Ohio.

The Wright brothers demonstrate their airplane to the US Army at Ft. Myer, Virginia, September 1908

Portrait of **Henry VIII** by Hans Holbein the Younger. Henry VIII was excommunicated on December 17, 1538.

More December 17 Events

From the creation of great works of engineering and art, to devastating wars and natural disasters, thousands of years of history have left their mark on each and every day of the year. Here are some important events that occurred on December 17. (Illustrated items are shaded.)

546 — After a siege of nearly a year, **Rome is sacked** by the Ostrogoths, who plunder the city.

1538 — **Henry VIII of England is excommunicated** from the Catholic Church by Pope Paul III for his marriage to Anne Boleyn. (The actual excommunication took place in 1533 under Pope Clement VII, but was not made official until later.)

1790 — The **Aztec calendar stone** is discovered in Mexico City.

Aztec calendar stone (Photo: Anagoria, CC BY-SA 3.0)

1862 — Union General Ulysses S. Grant issues **General Order No. 11,** expelling all Jews in Tennessee, Mississippi, and Kentucky. The order was revoked by Abraham Lincoln in January of the following year.

1865 — Franz Schubert's **"Unfinished Symphony"** (Symphony No. 8) has its premier performance of the completed movements.

1892 — The first issue of *Vogue* magazine is published.

1935 — The **Douglas DC-3** makes its first flight. Over 16,000 will be produced (including the military C-47 version), of which 2,000 are still in service as of 2013.

Douglas DC-3 "Sleeper Transport" version, the first type built
(Photo: Bill Larkins, CC BY-SA 2.0)

1943 — With the passage of the **Magnuson Act**, Chinese immigration is allowed into the US for the first time since 1882, and resident Chinese are allowed to become naturalized citizens.

1944 — During World War II's Battle of the Bulge, the **Malmedy massacre** of 84 American POWs by members of the 1st SS Panzer Division takes place.

1951 — The US Civil Rights Congress presents the report "**We Charge Genocide**: The Crime of Government Against the Negro People" to the United Nations. The report is suppressed in the US because of supposed Communist influence and leaders of the organization are barred from traveling internationally.

1969 — The US Air Force **Project Blue Book** study of unidentified flying objects (UFOs) is officially terminated.

1989 — The animated sitcom *The Simpsons* premiers on television. It will become the longest-running American scripted primetime television series, with over 600 episodes released at the time of writing.

2003 — The air-launched rocket powered aircraft **SpaceShipOne** achieves supersonic flight for the first time on the hundredth anniversary of the Wright brothers flight.

2014 — The US and Cuba re-establish diplomatic relations after 54 years.

Quote of the Day

"You were born with wings. Why prefer to crawl through life?"

Jalal al-Din Muhammad Rumi (جلالالدين محمد رومی)
Sufi philosopher, theologian, and poet
died December 17, 1273

Births
and
Deaths
THER
ACA
MAGNA
December 17

Pope Francis, 266th pope of the Roman Catholic Church, born
December 17, 1936; elected March 13, 2013. (Photo: Casa
Rosada, Argentina Presidency of the Nation, CC BY-SA 2.0)

Notable December 17 People

With the current world population at about seven billion people, on average about 19 million people also celebrate their birthdays on December 17 — and that isn't counting millions and millions who came before! No matter when you were born, you share your birthday with many special people whose accomplishments (and occasionally embarrassments) have been noted as part of history.

In this section, you'll meet fascinating people who share your birthday. They're organized by what they're famous for, and then in reverse chronological order from most recent to earliest. Those who are shown in photographs or artwork have a box around them. We don't have photos of everyone, so please forgive us if your favorite person is missing.

Some of these people you've heard of, others will be new to you, but they all make up an important part of the reason that December 17 is a truly special day!

 Michael Dobson

John Greenleaf Whittier, poet, born December 17, 1807

Who Was Born on December 17?

Business

Burt Baskin, co-founded the Baskin-Robbins ice cream chain with his brother-in-law Irv Robbins. *(1913)*

Journalism and Publishing

Chris Matthews, television journalist best known for his MSNBC talk show *Hardball With Chris Matthews.* *(1945)*

Bob Guccione, founded the adult magazine *Penthouse. (1930)*

William Safire, Presidential speechwriter, journalist, and television commentator known for creating the phrase "nattering nabobs of negativism" for Spiro Agnew, and for his witty "On Language" column in *The New York Times Magazine. (1929)*

Literature and Poetry

Jacqueline Wilson, children's writer best known for her *Tracy Beaker* novels. *(1945)*

Jack L. Chalker, science fiction writer best known for his "Well World" series. *(1944)*

John Kennedy Toole, New Orleans writer best known for his Pulitzer Prize-winning posthumous novel *A Confederacy of Dunces.* (1937)

Penelope Fitzgerald, award-winning author listed by the *Times of London* as one of the greatest British writers of the post-war era, best known for her novels *The Blue Flower* and *The Golden Child.* (1916)

Erskine Caldwell, American writer known for his writings about poverty and racism in the American South; best known for his novels *Tobacco Road* and *God's Little Acre*, both made into films. (1903)

Ford Madox Ford, English writer best known for his 1915 novel *The Good Soldier,* often cited as one of the best novels of the 20th century, and the *Parade's End* tetralogy, adapted into a BBC/HBO miniseries in 2012. (1873)

John Greenleaf Whittier, American Quaker poet and abolitionist whose best known works are *Barbara Frietchie* ("'Shoot, if you must, this old gray head / But spare your country's flag,' she said.") and *Barefoot Boy* ("Blessings on thee, little man / Barefoot boy, with cheek of tan!"). (1807) *(Photo page 20.)*

Military

Chelsea Manning, US Army trans soldier (born Bradley Manning) convicted of leaking 750,000 classified or sensitive documents to WikiLeaks. (1987)

Simo Häyhä, Finnish sniper credited with 505 kills against Red Army forces in the 1939-1940 Winter War, the highest number of confirmed sniper kills in any major war. *(1905)*

Simo Häyä

The Temptations (left to right): Otis Williams, Melvin Franklin, **Eddie Kendricks**, Paul Williams, and Dennis Edwards

Music

Tracy Byrd, country music singer of the 1993 number #1 hit "Holdin' Heaven." *(1966)*

Bob Stinson, founding member and lead guitarist of The Replacements. *(1959)*

Mike Mills, founding member of the alt-rock group R.E.M. *(1958)*

Paul Rodgers, singer-songwriter known for his work with Bad Company and Queen; listed by Rolling Stone as one of the "100 Greatest Singers of All Time;" hits include "All Right Now," "Feel LIke Makin' Love," and "These Arms of Mine." *(1949)*

Paul Butterfield, blues harmonica player and singer best known for headlining the Paul Butterfield Blues Band; member of the Blues Hall of Fame and the Rock and Roll Hall of Fame. *(1942)*

Eddie Kendricks, singer-songwriter who co-founded The Temptations; lead voice on such hits as "The Way You Do The Things You Do," "Get Ready," and "Just My Imagination (Running Away With Me)." *(1939)*

James Booker, New Orleans rhythm and blues musician known as the "Black Liberace" for his flamboyant stage personality. *(1939)*

Tommy Steele, Britain's first teen rock and roll star known for his 1957 number one hit "Singing the Blues," also appeared in such films as *Half a Sixpence* and *Finian's Rainbow.* *(1936)*

Sy Oliver, jazz arranger, bandleader, and trumpeter known for his work with Ella Fitzgerald, including co-writing the hit "T'aint What You Do (It's the Way That You Do It," and as one of the first African Americans featured in a white band with Tommy Dorsey, for whom he arranged the hit "On the Sunny Side of the Street." *(1910)*

Arthur Fiedler, conductor of the Boston Pops Orchestra for half a century; featured on the long-running PBS program *Evening at Pops*; received the Presidential Medal of Freedom. *(1894)*

Performing Arts

Nat Wolff, actor and musician who composed the music for an co-starred in the Nickelodeon television series *The Naked Brothers Band. (1994)*

Emma Bell, actress who played Amy, younger sister of Laurie Holden's character Andrea in *The Walking Dead. (1986)*

Milla Jovovich, actress in *The Fifth Element, The Messenger: The Story of Joan of Arc, Resident Evil,* and others. *(1975)*

Rian Johnson, writer and director of *Star Wars: The Last Jedi,* eighth film in the *Star Wars* franchise. *(1973)*

Laurie Holden, played Andrea, older sister of Emma Bell's character Amy in the television series *The Walking Dead* and Adele in the film *Dumb and Dumber To. (1969)*

Peter Farrelly, filmmaker with his brother Bobby Farrelly; films include *Dumb and Dumber, Kingpin, Shallow Hal,* and others. *(1956)*

Bill Pullman, starred in such films as *Spaceballs, The Accidental Tourist, While You Were Sleeping,* and *Independence Day. (1953)*

Bill Pullman (Photo: Eye Steel Film, CC BY-SA 2.0)

The cast of *The Partridge Family*. Standing, l-r, David Cassidy, Susan Dey, **Dave Madden;** sitting l-r, Danny Bonaduce, Shirley Jones, Jeremy Gelbwaks, and (front left) Susanne Crough

Eugene Levy, comedian and filmmaker best known for his work on the sketch comedy series *SCTV* and as Noah in the *American Pie* franchise. *(1946)*

Ernie Hudson, actor best known for playing Winston Zeddemore in the *Ghostbusters* film series. *(1945)*

Bernard Hill, actor known for playing Captain Smith in the 1997 film *Titanic*, Théoden in the *Lord of the Rings* films, and the warden in Clint Eastwood's *True Crime*. *(1944)*

María Elena Velasco, Mexican actress and filmmaker best known for creating and portraying the character "La India Maria." *(1940)*

Dave Madden, actor primarily known for playing Reuben Kincaid on the 1970s sitcom *The Partridge Family*. *(1931)*

Richard Long, actor known for the television series *The Big Valley, Nanny and the Professor, Bourbon Street Beat,* and *77 Sunset Strip*. *(1927)*

Religion

Pope Francis, elected Pope of the Roman Catholic Church in 2013; the first Jesuit pope, the first from the Americas, the first from the Southern Hemisphere, and the first to choose a name not used by a predecessor since 913 CE. *(1936) (Photo page 18.)*

Science and Mathematics

Kenneth E. Iverson, received the Turing Award for his pioneering work in computer science, most notably the development of the APL programming language. *(1920)*

Willard Libby, awarded the 1960 Nobel Prize in Chemistry for his role in the development of radiocarbon dating. *(1908)*

Joseph Henry, first Secretary of the Smithsonian Institution and a scientist who developed the electromagnet as a practical device. The standard unit of inductance, the Henry, is named for him. *(1797)*

Sir Humphry Davy, pioneering chemist and inventor who isolated a number of elements for the first time. He invented the Davy Lamp, a safety lamp for use in coal mines, and an early precursor to the incandescent light bulb . *(1778)*

Sports

Chuck Liddell, mixed martial artist who helped bring MMA into mainstream American sports; member of the UFC Hall of Fame. *(1969)*

Bob Ojeda, baseball pitcher known as part of the 1986 World Series starting rotation of the New York Mets, and for surviving a 1993 boating accident that killed fellow pitchers Steve Olin and Tim Crews. *(1957)*

Sir Humphry Davy, by Sir Thomas Lawrence

Peter Snell, New Zealand runner who won three gold medals in the 1960 and 1964 Olympic Games; received a knighthood and was named to the International Association of Athletics Federations Hall of Fame. *(1938)*

Kerry Packer, Australian media tycoon best known for founding World Series Cricket. *(1937)*

Cal Ripken Sr., coach and manager for the Baltimore Orioles for 36 years; several of his players, including Jim Palmer, Eddie Murray, and his son Cal Ripken, Jr., had Hall of Fame careers. *(1935)*

Cal Ripken, Sr. (left) and Cal Ripken, Jr.

Loren Murchison, American sprinter who won gold medals in the 1920 and 1924 Olympic Games. *(1898)*

Gerald Patterson, Australian tennis player ranked World No. 1 in 1919; member of the International Tennis Hall of Fame. *(1895)*

Sam Barry, college athletic coach who achieved successes in football, baseball, and basketball primarily for the University of Southern California; member of the Naismith Memorial Basketball Hall of Fame and the College Basketball Hall of Fame. *(1892)*

Loren Murchison (Photo: Underwood Press)

Simón Bolivar, by M. N. Bate

Who Died on December 17?

Person of the Day
1830 — Simón Bolivar

Simón Bolivar, known throughout South America as *El Libertador,* was a military and political leader who played a major role in the estalishment of Venezuela, Bolivia, Colombia, Ecuador, Peru, and Panama as independent sovereign nations free of Spanish rule.

Born in what is now Venezuela on July 24, 1783, Bolivar attended military academies in Caracas and Madrid, then moved to France where he witnessed the coronation of Emperor Napoleon.

He returned to South America, where he became a military leader in the independence struggle. His decisive victory at the Battle of Carabobo in 1821 resulted in the creation of the state of Gran Colombia (modern Colombia, Ecuador, Panama, and Venezuela), with Bolivar as president.

Following his victory at the Battle of Junin in 1824, he also created the Confederation of the Andes (Peru and Bolivia). He hoped to achieve a permanent consolidation of Spanish-speaking South America into a single nation.

Unfortunately, he was unsuccessful. Internal struggles and civil wars tore apart the nation he had created, and in 1830, Bolivar stepped down from the presidency, saying "I ask you, beg you, to remain united, lest you become the assassins of the country and your own executioners."

Gran Colombia did not long survive his departure, dissolving later that year.

Believing that "all who served the revolution have plowed the sea," Bolivar planned to go into exile in Europe. Before he could set sail, he contracted tuberculosis, and died December 17, 1830, at the age of 47.

Although his authoritarian and militaristic views have been criticized, Bolivar remains a hero throughout the region, cited by many governmental leaders of all stripes as an inspiration. The nation of Bolivia is named for him, and the official name of Venezuela is the Bolivarian Republic of Venezuela, also in his honor. Currencies of both nations (the boliviano and the bolivar) are named for him, as are numerous cities, statues, and buildings.

Simón Bolivar leading his troops at the Battle of Junin, August 1824, painting by Martín Tovar y Tovar

Other December 17 Deaths

Art and Photography

Frank Rinehart, artist famous for his portrait photographs of Native American personalities and scenes. *(1928)*

Apache chief Geronimo, photographed by **Frank Rinehart**

Government

Daniel Inouye, US Senator from Hawaii for fifty years and highest-ranking Japanese-American politician in US history; won the Medal of Honor during World War II. *(2012)*

Kim Jong-il (김정일**),** "dear leader" of North Korea from 1994 until his death. *(2011)*

Leopold II of Belgium, second King of Belgium, best known for claiming the Congo (now the Democratic Republic of the Congo) as his private property; around 10 million Congolese people died under his regime. *(1909)*

Marie Louise, Duchess of Parma, Austrian archduchess who became Empress of the French as the second wife of Napoleon; given rulership over the duchies of Parma, Piacenza, and Guastalla until her death. *(1847)*

Literature and Journalism

Jack Anderson, Pulitzer Prize-winning investigative journalist whose major stories included exposing Nixon administration harassment of John Lennon, fugitive Nazis in South America, CIA plots to assassinate Fidel Castro, and exposing the Iran-Contra affair under President Reagan. He was famously targeted for assassination by the White House "plumbers" group for his investigations into Watergate. *(2005)*

Empress Marie Louise, by François Gérard (1810)

Kaspar Hauser, by Johann Georg Laminit

Dorothy L. Sayers, writer, poet, and translator; best known for her mystery series featuring Lord Peter Wimsey. *(1957)*

Music

Captain Beefheart, influential rock performer whose work integrated blues, rock, free jazz, and modern experimental composition. *(2010)*

Grover Washington, Jr., jazz funk and soul saxophonist who helped create the "smooth jazz" genre, best known for his hit with Bill Withers "Just the Two of Us." *(1999)*

Rex Allen, Western actor and musician known as "the Arizona Cowboy" and as narrator of a number of Disney nature films. *(1999)*

Mystery

Kaspar Hauser, feral child who first appeared as a teenager on the streets of Nuremberg, Germany, who claimed to have been raised in a dungeon; died mysteriously of stab wounds, the source of which are unknown. *(1833)*

Performing Arts

Jennifer Jones, star during the 1940s, won an Oscar for her role in the 1943 film *The Song of Bernadette.* *(2009)*

Dana Andrews, film star in the 1940s whose best known roles were in the films *Laura* and *The Best Years of Our Lives. (1992)*

Dana Andrews

Thomas Mitchell, actor who played Scarlett's father in *Gone With the Wind*, Doc Boone in *Stagecoach*, and Uncle Billy in *It's a Wonderful Life*; first actor to win an Oscar, an Emmy, and a Tony Award. *(1962)*

Eddie Acuff, actor best known for playing the postman in the *Blondie* film series of the 1930s and 1940s. *(1928)*

Religion

Jalal al-Din Muhammad Rumi (جلالالدين محمد رومی), commonly known as Rumi, was a Sufi philosopher and theologian, as well as one of the world's most popular poets. His best known works are the *Maṭnawīye Ma'nawī* (*Spiritual Couplets*; مثنوی معنوی), and the *Dīvān-e Šams-e Tabrīzī* (*The Works of Šams Tabrīzī*; ديوان شمس تبريزی). *(1273)*

Science and Medicine

Henry Heimlich, surgeon and researcher best known for developing the Heimlich maneuver for stopping choking. *(2016)*

Victor Franz Hess, received the 1936 Nobel Prize in Physics for the discovery of cosmic rays. *(1964)*

Elizabeth Garrett Anderson, first woman to qualify as a physician and surgeon in Britain, co-founded the first hospital staffed by women; also the first female dean of a British medical school, the first female doctor of medicine in France, and the first female mayor and magistrate in Britain. *(1917) (Photo page 44.)*

Elizabeth Garrett Anderson (Photo: Walery, Sampson Low & Co.)

William Thomson, 1st Baron Kelvin, Scots-Irish mathematical physicist and engineer who made major contributions to the field of thermodynamics; determined the lowest limit of temperature (absolute zero). The unit of measurement of absolute temperatures is named the Kelvin in his honor. *(1907)*

Sports

Sammy Baugh, quarterback for the Washington Redskins from 1937 to 1952; named to the Pro Football Hall of Fame. *(2008)*

Larry Sherry, relief pitcher for the Los Angeles Dodgers and Detroit Tigers, named MVP of the 1959 World Series. *(2006)*

Otto Graham, quarterback for the Cleveland Browns; named to the Pro Football Hall of Fame. *(2003)*

1954 Bowman Gum card of Otto Graham

Quote of the Day

"If I've told you once, I've told you a million times — resist hyperbole."

William Safire, journalist
born December 17, 1929

Holidays
Around
the World

THERI ACC MAGNA

December 17

Ugyen Wangchuck, first Druk Gyalpo of Bhutan (center, standing), along with his family, 1905 — for the **National Day of Bhutan**

December 17 Events

If you're looking for a reason to take your special day off, you should know that every single day is a holiday somewhere in the world! Here's some of what you can celebrate on December 17!

General Events

Accession Day (Bahrain)

The eastern Arabian nation of Bahrain observes the beginning of the reign of its first Emir, Isa bin Salman Al Khalifa (عيسى بن سلمان آل خليفة) on December 17, 1961.

Flag Day (Kurdish people)

The Kurdish independence movement celebrates the creation of its flag on December 17, 1999, by dancing, eating, and celebrating.

International Day to End Violence Against Sex Workers (worldwide)

Originally a memorial and vigil for the victims of Seattle's Green River Killer, this day calls attention to hate crimes committed against sex workers worldwide.

National Day (Bhutan)

The South Asian nation of Bhutan celebrates December 17 as a public holiday, commemorating the coronation of the first Druk Gyalpo (king) of modern Bhutan, Ugyen Wangchuck, on December 17, 1907.

Pan American Aviation Day (US)

By Act of Congress, the United States observes Pan American Aviation Day on the anniversary of the first Wright brothers flight on December 17, 1903, to promote aviation to promote development and communication among nations in the Western Hemisphere.

Wright Brothers Day (US, Ohio)

US President Dwight D. Eisenhower first established Wright Brothers Day on December 17. It is also observed as an official commemoration in Ohio, the home of the Wrights. *(See page 9.)*

Wilbur and Orville Wright are young Ohio men who have invented a flying machine that really flies. Their airship has been successfully navigated at Kitty Hawk, N. C. The young men are the sons of Bishop Milton Wright of Dayton, O.

Article from *The Tacoma Times*, December 26, 1903

Food Days

In the United States, almost every day of the year is dedicated to a particular food. (Some other countries also have official food days, but only in America is there one every single day!) Sponsored by manufacturers, retailers, farmers, or simply fans, these days are often proclaimed by the President, Congress, state governors, or mayors. Given that there are more different foods than days of the year, some days honor more than one kind of food!

In the US, December 17 is **National Maple Syrup Day.** Maple syrup is made by drilling holes into the trunks of maple trees and collecting the sap, which is then heated to evaporate most of the water, leaving behind concentrated syrup.

A bottle of maple syrup (Photo: Miguel Andrade)

Maple syrup was first made by Native Americans, and later adopted by European settlers. Today, the province of Quebec in Canada produces more than 8 million gallons (30 million liters) of maple syrup per year, nearly 70% of the world's output.

Vermont is the largest producer of maple syrup in the US, responsible for about 6% of the world's supply, or about 1.3 million gallons (5 million liters). Small amounts of maple syrup are produced in Japan and South Korea. (South Koreans prefer the maple sap before it's turned into syrup.)

Maple syrup is frequently added to breakfast foods, such as pancakes, waffles, or oatmeal. It's also used in baking as a sweetner.

"Sugar-Making Among the Indians in the North," by William De La Montagne Cary (Canadian Illustrated News, 1883) for **National Maple Syrup Day**

Food Months

In addition, the entire month of December is used to celebrate numerous foods.With Christmas on the horizon, it shouldn't be surprising that December is ! **National Egg Nog Month, National Fruit Cake Month,** and **National Pear Month**.

December is also **Food Service Safety Month**. That's probably why the first week in December is **National Handwashing Week**.

Grapes, Lemons, Pears, and Apples, by Vincent van Gogh — for **National Pear Month**

Religious Feast Days and Holidays

Hanukkah (חֲנֻכָּה) (Judaism)
The Jewish celebration of Hanukkah, also known as
the Festival of Lights or the Feast of Dedication,
takes place for eight days and nights beginning on
the 25th day of Kislev, which varies from late
November to late December. It commemorates the
rededication of the Second Temple in Jerusalem at
the time of the Maccabean Revolt.

Each night of Hanukkah is marked by lighting
one branch of the Menorah, a candelabrum with nine
branches. In addition to prayers, celebrants eat foods
fried or baked in olive oil. Children play with a
spinning top known as a *dreidel* and receive
Hanukkah gelt.

18th century painting of a Hanukkah celebration, artist unknown.

O Sapientia (Roman Catholics, Lutherans, Presbyterians)

The last seven days of Advent marked by antiphons sung or recited at church services from December 17 to December 23, known as the "O Antiphons." Each antiphon is a name of Christ based on attributes mentioned in Scripture. December 17 is "O Sapientia," or "O Wisdom."

Saint Days

Each day in the year is considered a feast day for one or more saints. They are somewhat different in western Christianity (Catholicism and many forms of Protestantism) and in eastern (Orthodox) Christianity.

In *Western Christianity*, December 17 is the feast day of Saints Daniel the Prophet, Josep Manyanet i Vives, Lazarus of Bethany (in Cuba), Olympia the Deaconess, Wivina, and Sturm.

In *Eastern Orthodox Christianity*, it is also the commemoration of Saints Athanasius, Nicholas, Anthony, Maxentiolus, Tydecho of Wales, Briarch, Judicaël, Begga, Eigil of Fulda, Dionysios of Zakynthos, and Misael of Abalatsk. (These saints are honored on December 4 by "Old Calendrists. *")

---

* "Old Calendrists" use the Julian calendar rather than the modern Gregorian calendar. December 17 on the Gregorian calendar is the same as December 4 on the Julian calendar. See "What Day of the Week is December 17?"

Honorary Months and Moveable Celebrations

Presidents, Congresses, and nations around the world issue proclamations recognizing particular months to honor certain causes. These events generally fall in December, though honorary months do come and go. If not otherwise specified, all months are US. Here are some honorary designations for December.

- Bingo's Birthday Month (the game, not the dog)
- National Critical Infrastructure Protection Month
- National Impaired Driving Prevention Month
- National Sign Up for Summer Camp Month
- National Stress-Free Family Holiday Month
- National Tie Month
- No Gender December
- Safe Toys and Gifts Month
- Spiritual Literacy Month
- Universal Human Rights Month
- Write a Business Plan Month

Just for Fun

The third Friday of December is celebrated as **Underdog Day**, honoring unsung heroes, runners up, and unlikely winners in all fields.

An "underdog," originally, worked in a shipbuilding yard, standing in a dark pit to help saw planks of wood along with the "overdog," who stood above. The underdog got covered with sweat and sawdust, while the overdog got all the credit.

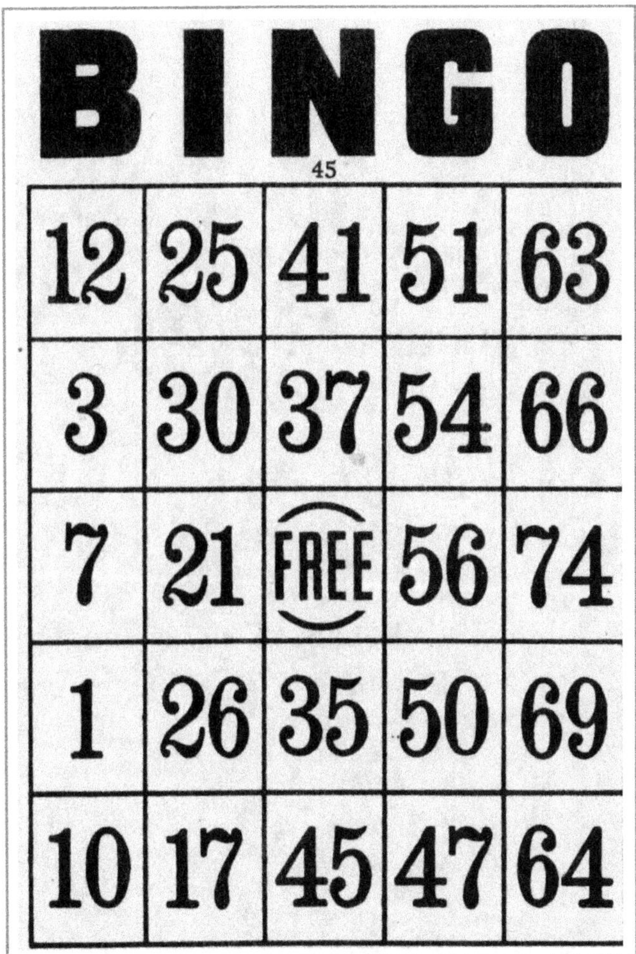

Bingo card (Photo: Abbey Hendrickson, CC BY-SA 2.0) — for **Bingo's Birthday Month**

Quote of the Day

"Ooh, with a little luck —
December will be magic again."

Kate Bush, singer-songwriter
"December Will be Magic Again"

About
the
Month
of
December

　Michael Dobson

"December," from the *Brevarium Grimani* by Simon Bening (c.1510)

December: The Twelfth Month

"In cold December fragrant chaplets blow,
And heavy harvests nod beneath the snow."

— Alexander Pope, *Dunciad.*

In Latin, *decem* means "ten," so it may seem strange that December is actually the twelfth month of the year. The original Roman calendar, from which our month names come, began in March, making December indeed the tenth month.

No one is completely sure when the start of the year was moved to January, but the traditional name of December stuck.

In the northern hemisphere, December is the month with the shortest daylight hours of the year; in the southern hemisphere, it's the opposite. December is the equivalent of June in the southern hemisphere, and vice versa.

In the Julian and Gregorian calendars, December is the twelfth and last month of the year, and is one of seven months with 31 days.

In every year, December starts on the same day of the week as September, and ends on the same day of the week as April.

The length of the day varies through the year, because the Earth tilts as it revolves around the Sun. The two extremes are known as the *solstices*, and the points at which day and night are of equal length are known as the *equinoxes*. The northern hemisphere's winter solstice, which is the shortest day of the year, falls in December. In the southern hemisphere, the summer solstice, the longest day of the year, falls in December.

The dates of the solstice can vary between December 20 and 22. Because even the ancients could tell when the days stopped getting shorter (or longer) and started in the other direction, many holidays and festivals take place around the time of the solstice, including most famously Christmas.

"December," by a follower of Cornelis Troost

December in Other Cultures

In Albanian, the month of December is known as *Dhjetor*. In Egyptian Arabic, it's ديسمبر (pronounced *dīsambar*). In Czech, it's *Prosinec*, in Finland it's *Joulukuu*, and in Poland it's *Grudzień*. Hungarians say *Karácsony hava*.

In Greek, the month of Δεκέμβριος is pronounced *Dekémbrios*. In Hebrew, it's דצמבר and Hindi, it's दसिंबर.

In Irish Gaelic, the month of December is *Nollaig mi na Nollag* and in Scottish Gaelic it's *an Dùbhlachd*. The Welsh say *Rhagfyr*.

The Chinese and Japanese both write the month 十二月, but it is pronounced differently in Cantonese, Mandarin, and Japanese. Koreans write it as 십이월, or *Sipiweol*. In Vietnam it's 腩迏乚 (*Tháng mười hai*).

In Old English, the month is *Gēolmōnaþ* and in Anglo-Saxon it's *Ærra-ġēola mōnaþ*.

The month of December does not correspond exactly with months in other calendar systems. The Hebrew months of כִּסְלֵו (*Kislev*) and טֵבֵת (*Tevet*) overlap December, as do the Persian months of آذر (*Azar*) and دی (*Dey*) and the Hindu months of मार्गशीर्ष (*Mārgaśirṣa*) and पूस (*Pauṣa*).

In the Islamic world, the lunar calendar consists of 354 or 355 days, meaning that the months slowly migrate through the year, and over time different months correspond to December.

December Sayings and Superstitions

- "A green December fills the graveyard."
- "When December snows fall fast, marry and true love will last."
- "A December bride will be fond of novelty, entertaining but extravagant."
- "Married in days of December's cheer / Love's star shines brighter from year to year."

Which day should you marry? That's easy.

"Monday for health
Tuesday for wealth
Wednesday best of all
Thursday for losses
Friday for crosses
Saturday for no luck at all."

According to legend, auspicious dates for December weddings are 1, 8, 10, 19, 23, and 29.

December Birthstones and Flowers

Birthstone: December birthstones in various traditions include turquoise, lapiz lazuli, zircon, blue topaz, and tanzanite.

Oil painting on lapis lazuli, *Perseus Rescuing Andromeda*, by Giuseppe Cesari.

Birth Flowers: December's flowers are the narcissus and holly.

Illustration of holly by Anton Hartinger, *Atlas der Alpenflora* (1882)

"December," by Eugène Grasset

  Michael Dobson

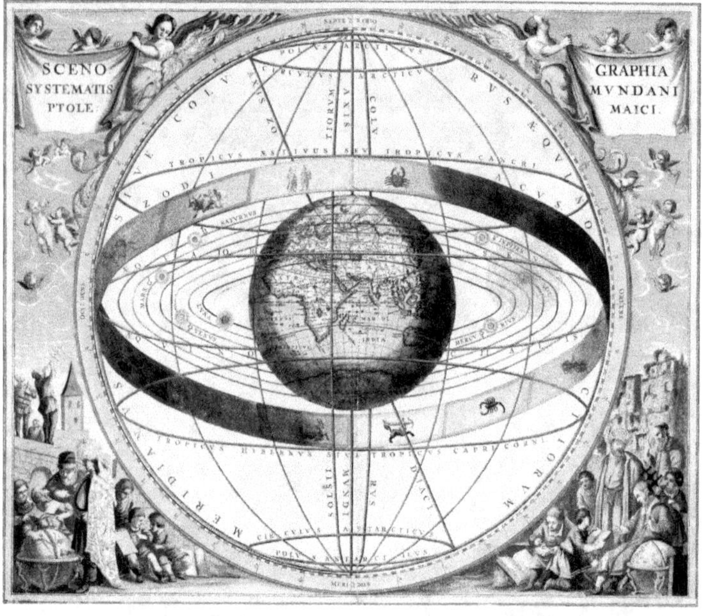

Scenography of the Ptolemaic Cosmography, by Johannes van Loon, based on Andreas Cellarius's *Harmonia Macrocosmica,* 1660

December 17 Zodiac Signs

From the perspective of someone on Earth, the Sun appears to move through the sky throughout the year, along a path astronomers call the *ecliptic plane*. The ecliptic plane is divided into twelve constellations, known as the zodiac, based on traditionally observed patterns of stars. On your birthday, you can't see your constellation, because it's in the daytime sky.

The zodiac was first developed by Babylonian astronomers about 2,500 years ago. Because they were unaware that the Earth wobbles like a spinning top (known as *precession*), they didn't make allowance for the fact that the Sun's path through the zodiac changes over time.

That means there are now two sets of dates for your birth sign. The *tropical dates* are the original Babylonian dates; the *sidereal dates* tell you where the Sun actually appears as it moves along its annual path.

December 17, however, is one of the few days of the year in which both the tropical and sidereal signs are the same: **Sagittarius.**

Sagittarius

Tropical November 23 to December 21
Sidereal December 16 to January 14

Sagittarius means "archer" in Latin. The constellation in the night sky is often depicted as having the appearance of a stick-figure archer drawing its bow.

The brighter stars in Sagittarius form an asterism known as The Teapot. The Milky Way is densest in Sagittarius, because the galactic center lies in that direction.

In astrology, Sagittarius is a fire sign. People born under it are said to be not superstitious. They are supposed to be drawn toward travel and philosophy, and to enjoy social contacts, meeting new people, and exploring other cultures. They are also said to be highly intelligent, visionary, and tolerant.

Sagittarians are considered compatible with Aries, Leo, and Gemini, and to a lesser extent with Taurus and Virgo.

Sagittarius, by Giovanni Maria Falconetto

Illustration by Edward Penfield

What Day of the Week is December 17?

On what day of the week does December 17 fall?

Surprisingly, this isn't an easy question. Because the calendar year is 365 days long (366 in leap years), it doesn't divide evenly by the seven days of the week.

Also, the Earth goes around the Sun in about 365-1/4 days, so a calendar tends to drift over time. That's why the same date falls on different weekdays in different years.

This is made even more complicated by a change in calendars that took place in 1582. Our modern calendar has its roots in ancient Rome, in a calendar reform conducted by Julius Caesar. Caesar commissioned mathematicians to attack the problem, and they came up with the idea of leap years, and thus standardized the calendar for centuries to come. This was called the Julian calendar.

Over time, however, the small errors in Caesar's calculation compounded. That's why Pope Gregory XIII commissioned the Gregorian calendar, used in most of the world today. Some countries converted in 1582, when the calendar was first developed; some converted later; other still haven't changed.

Gregorian and Julian aren't the only types of calendars. The Hebrew year, the Islamic year, and many other calendars are used in different parts of the world and among different people.

You can convert Gregorian dates to other calendars, including the Hebrew calendar, the Islamic calendar, and even the Mayan calendar by visiting the Fourmilab Calendar Converter at http://www.fourmilab.ch/documents/calendar/.

Chinese calendar systems are quite complex and have changed several times; a full discussion is far beyond the scope of this book. If you're interested, you can find information here: http://www.hermetic.ch/cal_stud/chinese_cal.htm.

On Names and Dates

Historians use "CE" (Common Era) and "BCE" (Before the Common Era) instead of the more common "AD" (Anno Domini, or Year of Our Lord) and "BC" (Before Christ), reflecting the fact that the year-numbering system established by the Gregorian calendar is used throughout the world in many countries not culturally Christian.

The CE/BCE designation dates back to at least 1708, and has been adopted as a standard by the United Nations and the Universal Postal Union. Because this series of books covers events and people of all nations and cultures, we use the CE/BCE terms.

The abbreviation "O.S." ("Old Style") and "N.S." ("New Style") on some dates refers to the fact that the Russian Empire (in particular) did not switch from the Julian to the Gregorian calendar at the same time as the rest of Europe, and therefore some figures and events have two dates.

Also, in the Julian calendar in England in the 16th century, the year began on March 25 rather than January 1. To avoid confusion with Gregorian dates, dates between January and March were often written using both years.

People and events whose original names are not in the Western alphabet have their native names (where possible) in the appropriate script shown in parenthesis. If you are using an e-reader to access an electronic version of this book, all characters don't always display on all devices.

A 50-year brass perpetual calendar.

Quote of the Day

"Time is an illusion, lunchtime doubly so."

Douglas Adams,
from *The Hitchhiker's Guide to the Galaxy*

Notes
and
Credits
Timespinner
Press

   Michael Dobson

Cartoon by John T. McCutcheon

Copyright, Credit, and Contact

Follow Us

Our blog "This Day in History" (http://
timespinnerpress.com/this-day-in-history/) features short
articles on events and people associated with each day, and
updates several times each week. Also subscribe to the
"Quote of the Day" at http://timespinnerpress.com/quote-
of-the-day/. You can get daily links by following us on
Facebook at TimespinnerPress, or on Twitter as
@sidewisethinker.

Contact Us

Find an error or a format problem? Want information about
the series, about us, or about when the volume for your
special day might be available? Please email us at
editor@timespinnerpress.com. (We also take requests if your
special day isn't yet complete. Please give us at least six
weeks' notice if possible.)

Sources

We owe a great debt to Wikipedia, which is our first stop for
research. We attempt to make independent confirmation of
all important dates and facts through a variety of other
sources.

Other sources we frequently use include the Library of
Congress; "on this day" listings from *Encyclopedia Britannica*,
the *New York Times*, and the BBC; Omniglot for the names of
months in other languages; *Chase's Calendar of Events*; and, of
course, the always essential Google.

All art and photographs are either in the public domain, used under a Creative Commons license, or with a "fair use" justification, and most frequently come from Wikimedia Commons and the Library of Congress Prints and Photographs Division.

Attribution is provided where possible, or as requested by the copyright owner, or when there is particular historical significance, listed below. For information about any particular illustration or photograph, please contact us.

Credits

1. The December 17, 1903, photograph of the first successful flight of the Wright Flyer was taken by John T. Daniels, and is from the collections of the Library of Congress, digital ID ppprs.00626. It is in the public domain because its first publication occurred prior to January 1, 1923.

2. The illustration of the month of December used on the back cover is from the French Gothic illuminated manuscript *Les Très Riches Heures du duc de Berry* by the Limbourg Brothers, Jean Colombe, and an intermediate painter whose name is lost to history. It is in the public domain because its copyright has expired.

3. The box graphic used on the first page is from a 1916 pamphlet entitled "Divorce versus Democracy" authored by G. K. Chesterton, originally published in London by the Society of St. Peter and St. Paul. It is in the public domain in the US because it was published prior to 1923, and is in the public domain in all countries (including the country of origin) in which the copyright time is the author's life plus 70 years or less.

4. The graphic design for the section pages in this book is from a design originally created for a pharmacy label. It is courtesy of Wellcome Images (ICV No 11073, photo V0010813), and is used here under CC BY-SA 4.0.

5. The painting "December" by Simon Bening was created circa 1510, and is in the public domain because its copyright has expired.

6. The 1908 postcard of the Wright brothers is in the public domain because its copyright has expired.

7. The October 10, 1902, photograph of the Wright brothers testing a glider at Kitty Hawk is in the public domain because its copyright has expired.

8. The 1908 photograph of a Wright Model A being flown at Ft. Myer, Virginia, is in the public domain as a work created by an employee of the US government as part of that person's official duties.

9. The portrait of Henry VIII of England by Hans Holbein the Younger was created circa 1540, and is in the public domain because its copyright has expired. It is in the Galleria Nazionale d'Arte Antica in Rome.

10. The 2013 photograph of the Aztec calendar stone is by Anagoria, and is used here under CC BY-SA 3.0.

11. The 2007 photograph of the Douglas Sleeper Transport (DC-3) is by Bill Larkins, and is used here under CC BY-SA 2.0.)

12. The 2015 photograph of Pope Francis is from the Casa Rosada (Argentine Presidency of the Nation) website (http://www.casarosada.gob.ar), and is used here under CC BY-SA 2.0 and CC BY-SA 2.5 Argentina.

13. The pre-1918 portrait of John Greenleaf Whittier is in the public domain because its copyright has expired.

14. The 1940 photograph of Simo Häyä is from the Finnish Military Archives. It is in the public domain in Finland, its country of origin, because it was first published before 1966. It is in the public domain in the US because it was published between 1923 and 1977 and without a copyright notice.

15. The 2011 photograph of Bill Pullman is from Eye Steel Film, Canada. It is used here under CC BY-SA 2.0.

16. The early 1970s publicity photo from *The Partridge Family* is in the public domain because it was published in the United States between 1923 and 1977 and without a copyright notice. Traditionally, publicity photographs are not copyrighted because of the way in which they are intended to be used.

17. The portrait of Sir Humphry Davy by Sir Thomas Lawrence was created prior to 1830, and is in the collection of the

National Portrait Gallery, London. It is in the public domain because its copyright has expired.

18. The 1982 publicity photograph of Cal Ripken Sr. and Jr. was released by the Baltimore Orioles. It is in the public domain because it was published in the United States between 1923 and 1977 and without a copyright notice.

19. The 1923 photograph of Loren Murchison was taken by Underwood Press. It is in the public domain because it was published in the United States between 1923 and 1977 and without a copyright notice.

20. The 1819 engraving of Simón Bolivar by M. N. Bate is in the public domain because its copyright has expired.

21. The 1824 painting "Batalla de Junín" by Martín Tovar y Tovar is in the public domain because its copyright has expired.

22. The 1898 photograph of Geronimo by Frank A. Rinehart is in the public domain because its copyright has expired.

23. The 1810 portrait of Empress Marie Louise by François Gérard is in the public domain because its copyright has expired.

24. The 1828/1829 drawing of Kaspar Hauser by Johann Georg Laminit is in the public domain because its copyright has expired.

25. The studio publicity photo of Dana Andrews is in the public domain because it was published in the United States between 1923 and 1977 and without a copyright notice. The image is from "Dana Andrews Pics," who has licensed it under CC BY-SA 3.0.

26. The 1889 photograph of Elizabeth Garrett Anderson is by Walery, and was first published by Sampson Low & Co. It is in the public domain because its copyright has expired.

27. The 1954 Bowman Gum card of Otto Graham is in the public domain because it was first published in the US between 1923 and 1963, and although there may or may not have been a copyright notice, the copyright was not renewed.

28. The 1905 photograph of Sir Ugyen Wangchuck and family is by John Claude White, courtesy British Library. It is in the public domain because its copyright has expired. The image has been cropped.

29. The article from the December 26, 1903, issue of *The Tacoma Times* is in the public domain because its copyright has expired.

30. The 2006 photograph of a bottle of maple syrup from Quebec, Canada, is by Miguel Andrade, who released it into the public domain.

31. The illustration "Sugar-Making Among the Indians in the North," by William De La Montagne Cary, first appeared in the May 12, 1883, issue of the *Canadian Illustrated News*. It is in the public domain because its copyright has expired.

32. The original 1887 painting "Grapes, Lemons, Pears, and Apples" by Vincent van Gogh is in the collection of the Art Institute of Chicago. The image is in the public domain because its copyright has expired.

33. The artist who created the 19th century painting of a Hanukkah celebration is unknown. The image is in the public domain because its copyright has expired.

34. The photograph of a bingo card was taken by Abbey Hendrickson, and is used here under CC BY-SA 2.0. It has been cropped.

35. The painting "December" is from the *Brevarium Grimani*, circa 1510, and is in the public domain because its copyright has expired.

36. The painting "December" by a follower of Cornelis Troost is from the 18th century, and is in the public domain because its copyright has expired.

37. The 1815 woodcut of a proposal is in the public domain because its copyright has expired.

38. The 16th century oil on lapis lazuli painting *Perseus Rescuing Andromeda* is by Giuseppe Cesari. It is in the public domain because its copyright has expired. The original object is in the collection of the Saint Louis Art Museum.

39. The 1882 painting of *Ilex aquifolium* (holly) is by Anton Hartinger, and appeared originally in the book *Atlas der Alpenflora*.

40. The 1896 drawing "December" by Eugène Grasset is in the public domain because its copyright has expired.

41. The celestial sphere is from *Scenography of the Ptolemaic Cosmography*, by Johannes van Loon, based on Andreas Cellarius's *Harmonia Macrocosmica*, 1660. It is in the public domain because its copyright has expired.

42. The fresco "Sign of Sagittarius" by Giovanni Maria Falconetto was created between 1515 and 1520, and is in the public domain because its copyright has expired. It is in the Palazzo d'Arco, Mantua, Italy.

43. The 1906 automobile calendar is by Edward Penfield, and is in the collection of the Library of Congress Prints and Photographs Division. It is in the public domain because its copyright has expired.

44. The 50-year perpetual calendar photograph is in the public domain.

45. The cartoon by John T. McCutcheon is from his 1905 collection *The Mysterious Stranger and Other Cartoons by John T. McCutcheon*. It is in the public domain because its copyright has expired.

46. The painting "December" by Joachim von Sandrart was created in 1642, and is in the public domain because its copyright has expired. The original can be found in the Schlossanlage Schleißheim, Germany.

47. The painting "December" by Hans Thoma is from his book *Festkalender*. It is in the public domain because its copyright has expired.

Timespinner
Press

License Description and Terms

Aside from material purely in the public domain, photographs and other material in this book are used under specific licenses permitting free use, usually with an attribution requirement. For full text and terms of these licenses, click or enter the appropriate links below. If you believe there is an error in the copyright status or attribution of any of these images, please email us.

- Creative Commons Attribution 2.0 Generic (CC-BY 2.0): http://creativecommons.org/licenses/by/2.0/deed.en
- Creative Commons Attribution-Share Alike 3.0 Generic (CC-BY-SA 3.0): http://creativecommons.org/licenses/by-sa/3.0/
- Creative Commons Attribution-Share Alike 2.5 Generic (CC-BY-SA 2.5): http://creativecommons.org/licenses/by-sa/2.5/deed.en
- Creative Commons Attribution-Share Alike 2.0 Generic (CC-BY-SA 2.0): http://creativecommons.org/licenses/by/2.0/deed.en
- Creative Commons Attribution-Share Alike 1.0 Generic (CC-BY-SA 1.0): http://creativecommons.org/licenses/by-sa/1.0/deed.en
- CC0 1.0 Universal (CC0 1.0) Public Domain Dedication (CC0 1.0) http://creativecommons.org/publicdomain/zero/1.0/deed.en
- GNU Free Documentation License (GFDL): http://en.wikipedia.org/wiki/Wikipedia:Text_of_the_GNU_Free_Documentation_License
- License Art Libre (Free Art License): http://artlibre.org

"December," by Joachim von Sandrart

Other Books from Timespinner Press

The Story of a Special Day
Michael Dobson

A series of (eventually) 366 volumes covering everything that happened on your special day! Events, births, deaths, quotes, holidays, and much more. It's like a birthday card they'll never throw away!

US$7.95 print/US$2.99 ebook.

From Plassey to Pakistan
Humayun Mirza

The history of British Colonial India and the formation of Pakistan from the unique perspective of the son of Pakistan's first president and last of the royal line of Bengal, Bihar, and Orissa! This unique historical document tells the inside story of this distinguished family, including the detailed story of the coup that toppled his father from power!

US$27.95 print

A Whole New Navy: America's War in the Pacific

Miles Durr

The most comprehensive and detailed description of America's naval war in the Pacific ever—every battle, every ship, every task force and every task group from Pearl Harbor through the Japanese surrender! A must-have for the collection of every World War II buff!

US$29.95 print

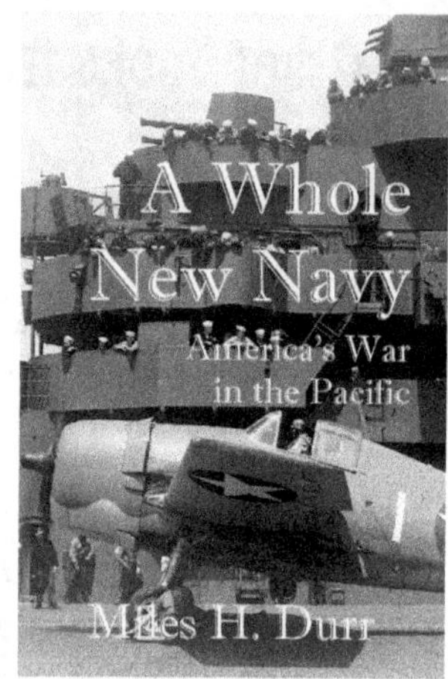

Improbable History: The Weird, the Obscure, and the Strangely Important

edited by Michael Dobson

From the birth of Western civilization to the rescue of Apollo 13, from the Leaning Tower of Pisa to Florence's Duomo, history has often turned on small, improbable details. Whatever happened to the ancient Samaritan people? Why did a fortuitous rainstorm allow the British to conquer India? How did an air raid in Italy lead to the development of chemotherapy? What happened when Albert Einstein met Adolf Hitler on the streets of Berlin? How did the Japanese manage to attack the US mainland using balloons? A cast of award-winning writers tackle some of the strangest tales in history!

US$19.95 print

The Letters of William Philip Schwartz 1842-1855

edited by John F. Schwartz

The 19th century soldier and adventurer William Philip Schwartz wrote a series of vivid and detailed letters chronicling his adventures in the Indian Wars, the Mexican-American War, the Gold Rush, and his term as Marine sergeant aboard the USS Constellation. A pioneer in photography, he took *the first known war photographs*. An unforgettable first-hand look into life in the 19th century!

US$17.95 print

Timespinner
Press

www.timespinnerpress.com

"December," from *Festkalendar,* by Hans Thoma

www.ingramcontent.com/pod-product-compliance
Lightning Source LLC
Chambersburg PA
CBHW060751260726
48660CB00002B/578